Who's Minding Your Mind?

'A Course in Miracles' concepts

Bette Jean Cundiff

Who's Minding Your Mind?

Copyright 2020

All rights reserved

Bette Jean Cundiff

ISBN: 9798647538475

bettejeancundiff.blogspot.com

Who's Minding Your Mind?

Lesson 1

The most powerful tool for the transformation of the world is at your disposal. Mind is the decision-maker, the powerhouse behind creativity. Mind takes you beyond daily experience into the realm of vision - and can make it come true. Mind is filled with emotional highs and lows, fears and joys, anger and forgiveness. Mind calms and mind destroys.

And mind is yours to use.

Let's get started with a little story:

Three employees walk into a bar together, a professor, a zombie and a monk.

Who's Minding Your Mind?

After they sit next to each other at the bar the bartender asks the professor, "What do you do?"

The professor myopically focuses on the bartender through thick glasses, and proudly answers, "I am an analyst. I research endlessly, compare one fact to another, and come to excruciating carefully debated and then logical conclusions. Analysis is I my life."

The bartender turns to the zombie and asks, "What do you do?"

The zombie rears forward toward the bartender, eyes rotating wildly in his scarred face. With saliva dripping from torn and bloody mouth he hisses at the bartender growling his answer, "What do I do?" he responds, his voice rising into a rant. "What do I do? You actually ask me what I do?" And he starts screaming now at the top of his lungs.

Who's Minding Your Mind?

"I REACT! That's what I DO!" And breathing heavily the zombie sits back down glaring wildly at the bartender.

The bartender, used to all sorts of characters who come into his bar just turns calmly to the final employee and asks, "What do you do?"

The monk serenely answers, "Nothing. I just am."

Then the bartender intrigued in spite of himself, asks them all one last question, "What company do you all work for?"

The professor sits up straighter, the zombie sneers and glares, hands on the counter ready to pounce, and the monk closes his eyes and gently smiles.

They answer together, "Your Mind."

Who's Minding Your Mind?

Thoughts to Contemplate and discuss

1. Take time to notice which part of your mind is prominently in charge during the day – the professor, the zombie or the monk. (This may not be as simple as you think because it will be easy to mislabel or ignore them.)

2. Are you willing to learn how to recognize more accurately who is in charge of your mind?

3. Are you willing to learn how to gain peaceful control of your mind?

If the answer is 'yes' to #2 and #3, then stick around and have fun and gain insight as you continue this course.

Who's Minding Your Mind?

Lesson 2

Mind over what...

...doesn't matter?

Many years ago, as I was giving a lecture to a spiritual group in the Midwest on the books entitled *A Course in Miracles*. I was asked a simple question, "Is this material teaching mind over matter?" I spontaneously answered with the response, "No, it is teaching mind over what doesn't matter!" Since then I have used this phrase many times, not just with my students and clients, but most especially with myself!

Boy, how seriously we take life. After all isn't being an adult judged by how responsibly we handle problems? And problems are serious business, right? Wrong!

"Wait," you say. "What do you mean problems aren't serious? I have lots of problems.

Who's Minding Your Mind?

My whole life is one insoluble problem - and I take this very seriously! I am responsible and I am an adult and this is no laughing matter!"

Whew! Bummer! What a drag! With this frame of reference every time we enjoy life we must feel unconsciously that we are irresponsible and immature. So naturally we are going to set ourselves up for more and more problems so that we can prove to ourselves and others how adult we are. If you doubt that this is true, just reflect for a moment or two on what you like to think about most of the time. And guess what you'll discover? You like to focus on your problems! You worry pretty consistently just to make sure you don't forget any of them. Gee, you wouldn't want to lose any, would you?

Does all this worry really make any difference? Not really. Rarely do we ever come up with solutions when we are so busy remembering, reliving and reorganizing our problems. So the obvious release from this imprisoning predicament

Who's Minding Your Mind?

is to shift from worry to serenity.

To move from worry to serenity effectively you will need to:

1. Shift beliefs about fun and adulthood.

2. Learn to focus on solutions rather than problems.

3. Discover what really matters and release what doesn't.

Being able to accomplish all three effectively takes time and tools, but hey, what else is time for?

Thoughts to contemplate and discuss

1. How seriously do you take life? Observe yourself over the next several days and notice how often you enjoy each moment and how often you are 'focused' intently on the issues in front of you with a slight frown. (That will give you a beginning clue on discovering your 'seriousness' level.
2. Do you find yourself repeating the problems challenging you to yourself and to others? (Here is a clue to whether you are focused on problems or answers)
3. Observe how easy it is for you to stop judging the issues and be willing to be 'wrong' in your assessment? (Hmmm, this is much easier said than done!)

Lesson 3

The Mirror Principle

As we continue, we will discover why all problems and pain come from the limited use of mind and the inability to discover a truly meaningful answer.

All pain comes from the initial erroneous belief in our sense of separation from Divinity. Our idea of separation from Totality, or God, and its resultant experience of limitation is an erroneous belief but one which seems vividly portrayed in the world around us - we feel misunderstood, victimized and attacked. This world seems to be based on isolation from an all powerful, protective and giving God. He may have all these aspects, but He seems not to be giving them to us.

Who's Minding Your Mind?

This concept of estrangement from God and Life did not start outside of ourseslves. It was not thrust upon us by the world or by God. On the contrary, the world merely reflects the beliefs we have chosen and now want to experience.

Let's look at how this works:

1. *Mind chooses a belief.*

Your beliefs are not thrust upon you! You choose what you believe is true. The mirror principle has five distinct steps. Once you take this first step the others will follow irrevocably.

2. *Belief is projected outward.*

Mind can't jealously contain anything! Its very nature means its thoughts are extended outward as an inter-dimensional, electromagnetic field. As has been stated before, "Thoughts are things and they have wings."

3. *Projection makes perception.*

Who's Minding Your Mind?

Once your mind chooses a belief, it projects this onto your life experiences. People, places, and events pass before you and your projected belief is reflected upon them. Your projections are now directing your perceptual experiences.

4. *Perception is a mirror, not a fact.*

Half a dozen witnesses to any accident will give half a dozen different perspectives when testifying. You see what you want to see based on your background, your training, and most importantly the beliefs you have chosen. You never experience the world - only your interpretation of it!

5. *What you see seems real.*

You use your senses to verify evidence. Yet your interpretation of your senses is based on a faulty system of perception. What you see only seems real, since it mirrors your original choice of belief. This is a closed system that is self-fulfilling.

Who's Minding Your Mind?

What Price Limitation?

Following this basic formula, you chose to think of the possibility of separation from God and the limitation of life. You projected out your thought and saw it mirrored around you in the world. Now your world seems to be filled with symbols of estrangement from God and limitations on life. The ultimate limitation is symbolized as death. You feel alone, vulnerable and victimized by outside forces. Every experience you have reinforces your basic belief "proving" that it is "true".

Is the concept of separation from God true? No! Is the concept of limitation of life possible? No! Totality and your shared Divinity cannot be changed or fragmented in any way. What you think and believe, however, can be erroneous. Each step in the mirror principle will irrevocably follow the one before, no matter what belief you start with. What you believe and think will be projected onto a neutral world coloring it with your ideas.

Who's Minding Your Mind?

Changing your beliefs is never easy because of your investment in them. You feel personally attacked if someone does not agree with your ideas. You will even attack yourself if you begin to question your own judgments! You believe that if you give up your beliefs you will give up the very essence of yourself. Your past experience has shown this to be accurate, for when you gave up the belief in your Divinity, you did lose touch with the essence of yourself. Now you must courageously let go of your beliefs once more - this time giving up limitation and separation. You will lose the essence of what you believe you are - limited, filled with pain, unworthy of any real happiness. How wonderful! And then you will be left with all that you forgot - Divinity, Life and Peace. The completeness of God's Love will be returned to your mind

Who's Minding Your Mind?

Thoughts to contemplate and discuss

1. Observe the many times each day you form opinions, judgments, and have prejudices for or against. For now, just acknowledge with each one that a pre-exiting belief was in place before you formed your viewpoints.
2. If you are ready to take the next step, you may want to create a list of the fundamental beliefs you have been taught throughout your life about relationships, the world and handling conflicts. Then look back at your insights in question 2 and see if you can find correlations.
3. Since giving up beliefs is very hard, let's start a real change by taking time to affirm throughout each day, "I may be very wrong about what I believe is going on." You may feel real resistance to this, but just repeating this is a huge step.

Lesson 4

Warning!

Your Survival Skills are Killing You!

The Whirling Vortex of Hell

You reject wisdom, fear love and defend yourself aggressively by finding fault in others. You equate this action as an attack on God for you refuse His gifts of guidance, love and peace. You believe you are a sinner. This thought is projected outward and the world, as well as God, reflects the idea of rejection and attack. You project your motives onto God and they are seen as His. You reason, "God must feel rejected and angry. He will demand vengeance and retaliation." The mirror principle which started with a belief in self-guilt leads directly to fear of God, of Life, of Love! The whirlpool has begun to suck you deeper into the vortex of emotional hell.

Not only God is seen through the mirror principle - the whole world is. You have rejected everyone and everything around you and expect them to be retaliatory. The viral infection of *victim-itis* has now been spawned. Guilt leads directly to the emotion of fear. You feel alone, unworthy, vulnerable and victimized

It seems easier to give up and be sucked down than to swim to the surface and survive.

Guilt, Fear and Anger – Tactics from Hell

This unbearably painful emotional state demands correction, but your logical mind, using the mirror principle as verification hatches a devious plot. Get rid of your pain by redirecting the wrath of God away from you. Do this by relentlessly searching out the faults in others. In

Who's Minding Your Mind?

other words, you project your own sense of guilt onto the world. This tactic is called anger. Anger points the finger of guilt away from you onto everyone and everything. Anger becomes your self protection from a vengeful God. Anger keeps the whirlpool spiraling downward, faster and faster.

I hope you have noticed there is, however, one major flaw in this logic. Anger is a form of attack on another and will lead directly to a renewed sense of self-guilt. The error began there in the first place. Self guilt brings fear of counter-attack and demands projections of blame. Thus the vicious cycle of separation, guilt, fear and anger that leads to more separation, guilt, fear and anger continues to swirl in perpetual motion.

Truth has become a commodity to be fought for, claimed and possessed. Whoever has the truth is all powerful and can command obedience. All will follow him who knows. In other words it's good to be a king! Until, of course your rivals challenge you for the crown.

Who's Minding Your Mind?

Thoughts to contemplate and discuss

1. When did you first hear that you were a sinner? If not, cool, but probably you have felt guilt and unworthiness at least a few times in your life, if not a few times each hour. Start with noticing how often this occurs and recognize the vortex is trying to suck you in.
2. Notice how often you feel irritated if not downright angry. Who are you angry with? Can you notice how important it is to make someone else wrong? Review the above paragraphs explaining this dynamic.
3. Take the time each day to want to be released of guilt, fear and anger. You only need to want this, the release will be done for you. (more on how this happens at another time)

Who's Minding Your Mind?

Lesson 5

The Battle for Truth

There are only two contestants in the battle for truth. Take a very close look at the side you have chosen. For you will back your choice, even with your life!

Contestant # 1

The Deadly Cycle

1. *DENIAL - The birth of all problems.*

The first step downward along the deadly cycle is the building up of walls. Denial keeps you from knowing the world, your relationships, yourself and God. You choose to separate rather than unify; to be blind rather than sighted. You no longer feel powerful, for you no longer feel connected to the spiritual Power that unites you with the Universe.

Who's Minding Your Mind?

2. *GUILT - The "original sin".*

You pay an astronomically high price for choosing denial - you lose your sense of worth. Refuse the gifts that God, life, the world, your relationships and even what you offer yourself, and you will feel like the Universe's biggest heel. All sense of unworthiness starts here. Guilt is born and breeds in the swamp of denial.

3. *FEAR - "Sin" demands punishment.*

The deadly cycle spirals downward and the belief in a basic unworthiness, or sinfulness, results in a logical assumption: Screw up and pay for it! Now the denied world, relationships, God, and even the denied aspects of yourself seem on the other side of an endless war zone. Terror grips your mind. You are surrounded by enemies.

Even Adam in the Garden of Eden knew ego's favorite tactic for self-preservation. When confronted by God, Adam pointed at Eve and

Who's Minding Your Mind?

whined, "She made me do it!" The world still relies on this ploy - blame someone else and the heats off you.

Anger is the best way to show your "innocence" by focusing on another's faults. Outwardly this seems to work, but inwardly the denied sense of guilt still festers and the need to constantly project anger onto others becomes an exhausting conflagration of battles. The Deadly Cycle continues downward into emotional hell.

If there is an "evil" in this world, then I submit that our own stubborn desire to continue the deadly cycle is "Satan" at work.

Do not be surprised if you feel some resistance to what you have read. As you contemplate these concepts, your loyalty to the first contestant, the Deadly Cycle, will cause it to flex its muscles and challenge you to a dual. Relax, reflect and remember what you have read.

Who's Minding Your Mind?

Thoughts to contemplate and discuss

1. Each time guilt builds within you, remember to use this affirmation, "I can feel my worth, instead of this."

2. Notice how often you find it important to be right and another person wrong. Notice how friends can bond over talking trash about an agreed upon target. ("A Course in Miracles" refers to these 'friendships' as special relationships)

3. Remind yourself that anger is a misguided attempt to make yourself feel innocent and another guilty. To counter act this, repeat the affirmation from question no. 1, above.

Who's Minding Your Mind?

Lesson 6

The Battle for Truth

Contestant # 2

The Healing Cycle

Shifting from the no/win dynamics of the Deadly Cycle to the win/win success of the Healing Cycle requires a simple change in mind. First, however, let's look at the Healing Cycle. Then we will explore how to shift from one cycle to another.

1. *ACCEPTANCE - Decision for wholeness*

Are you willing to be wrong? Are you willing to see things differently? Are you willing to look past the tip of your own disjointed nose to see a broader perspective, accept another opinion, listen to wisdom and advice? If your answer is "yes" then you have begun the first step upwards to healing and peace. You have begun the process of integration and union. You have begun to pull yourself together!

2. *WORTH - Forgiveness is the key.*

There are only one of two real messages that are sent from one to another, no matter the actual words used. The messages are:

a. "I am here to be helpful."

The response to this will naturally be gratitude.

b. "I am in desperate need of help."

The response to this will naturally be compassion.

All conversation boils down to the simple and profound - help being compassionately offered or help being gratefully accepted. This perspective on life is called being forgiving. And where can hate and anger be when only forgiveness is experienced?

3. *SAFETY - A little piece of Heaven on Earth.*

Just like the Starship Enterprise you, too, have a prime directive - offer a place of safety without intruding on the sacredness of other life forms and their choices. Everyone around you is struggling with the Deadly Cycle. Fear, obvious or disguised, runs the show. Your only responsibility is to respect the rights of others and by your acceptance and forgiveness demonstrate that they are the same as you and therefore safe.

4. *PEACE - Do you want to be right or happy?*

Pride is definitely one of the "deadly sins". So why not swallow a little bit of something that is invisible anyway, and end up with serenity. All war is a struggle to prove you know more than others. Free yourself by freeing others from the prison camp of arrogance. Then make the most important choice in your life - choose peace.

Who's Minding Your Mind?

Keep this in mind:

In the battle for truth your belief is the contestant that you have decided to back.

You are so highly invested in winning, you will support your belief even with your life!

This principle seems to offer a full - proof method to guarantee that your belief wins.

Thoughts to contemplate and discuss

1. Start internally translating all conversation with others into the two categories of real messages. See how easily you can see the call for help, or the offer of help in another's words. Be sure to notice the same in your own part of the conversation.

Who's Minding Your Mind?

2. Notice the real motive for your comments. Are you trying to prove you are right and not wrong at the expense of someone's comfort? If so, choose a comment that will make the other feel welcome and safe with you. If your motive is peace, then the right words will come.

3. A great quote from "A Course in Miracles" – "Do you want to be right or happy?" How important is it to win the argument if it ruins a relationship? You may find resistance to backing off. So may need to work hard at this one.

Who's Minding Your Mind?

Lesson 7

Into the Depths
Exploration and Discovery

Deep within ourselves is a pool, a reservoir of undeveloped and unexpressed ideas. Here is where our 'monk', who we met in the opening story, is ready to be of service to you. In our everyday experiences we rarely dip into this unending sea of wisdom allowing our inner monk to guide us. Yet, whether called the the Voice within, Universal Mind, or the Holy Spirit, this relatively untouched treasure house is ours to reach. Here is where the cold, hard facts of life must gently dissipate into a letting go of reason and a leaping into faith. No matter your spiritual beliefs this area of mind is there. Label it according to your comfort level, but

Who's Minding Your Mind?

remember, here is where insight and creativity emerge from the unconscious into expression.

Underneath all the hoopla surrounding the process of tapping into the reservoir is a simple technique begun with just one extremely challenging question, "Am I willing to surrender what my internal 'professor' of logic demands, and the clammering of the emotional dramas my zombie spews forth, to what my inner knowing, my 'monk,' offers?"

To reach this point in attitude takes some readjustment to how you approach your mind and the thinking process. You have been taught to trust your professor and use deductive reasoning, accumulate facts, information, advice and suggestions and then after due deliberation, reach a solution. So far so good. This has been and still is sound practice.

Or, we follow the zombie to become wrapped up in the seductive emotional reactions of guilt, fear and anger, which is not so good but always seem

Who's Minding Your Mind?

ridiculously important at the time.

The key will be, however, to sift through the often conflicting information and emotions and pluck out the wisdom hidden somewhere within. To do this the next step we need to access the monk.

There is no way to discover creative inspiration if you are unable to discern the monk's peaceful answer from the chaotic emotions of the zombie or the often times logical arguments of the professor churning within your mind. And so the process of learning to discern the differnces correctly between the advice offered by these three inner sources, must take some time and lots of practice.

Ultimately, accessing the monk is done through a process of willingness and meditation. And this must be your goal if you truly want to be the 'minder of your mind'.

<u>Who's Minding Your Mind?</u>

Thoughts to contemplate and discuss

1. So, if you haven't done so already, choose a course, a path, a teacher and go for it. There are many courses for guiding you through the tools and the practice necessary for success. "A Course in Miracles" is an excellent one.

2. Repeat a process suggested before but now with greater understanding. Observe the chatter in your mind and notice the professor's logic, the zombie's emotional dramas, and the monk's gentle gifts. Notice when each is comforting or creates chaos.

3. Take time each hour to stop, breath deeply and consciously choose to reach for the monk's gentle guidance.

Lesson 8

Three important points

1. YOU ARE POWERFUL

You are a child of the Most High. You are divinely royal by birthright. You do not have to fight to gain or maintain this title. All the rights, privileges and rewards of being divine are automatically yours. Because of Who your Parent is you naturally inherit all of Its qualities - you are Spirit, your mind is all encompassing, you have the ability to co-create, you lack nothing!

2. YOU HAVE RESPONSIBILITY

With the rights and privileges of divinity come the responsibility to use your power appropriately and wisely. Each day you awaken to a Universe that trembles with anticipation awaiting your divine direction and will respond to your slightest command. The order or chaos of a whole Universe and all within it are your responsibility!

3. YOU HAVE CHOICES TO MAKE

Your mind is under your control at all times. No one else can affect you. There are no evil energies sucking away your power like psychic vampires.

You can choose the Deadly Cycle all on your own and suffer the consequences.

Or you can choose the Healing Cycle and once more reclaim your divine title and crown.

Look for the other mini courses by Bette Jean Cundiff that help explain the complex concepts of "A Course in Miracles" in clear, fun and easy to understand format. You can find these on her webite at:

bettejeancundiff.blotspot.com

Who's Minding Your Mind?